Motivational Books:

365 Days of Positive Thinking:

A motivational quote-a-day to increase productivity and bring positive thinking into your life

365 Days of Motivation

Copyright © 2016 by Jenny Kellett

Cover by: Jenny Kellett

All rights reserved. No part of this book may be reproduced in any form by any electronic or mechanical means including photocopying, recording, or information storage and retrieval without permission in writing from the author.

ISBN-13: 978-1530549122

ISBN-10: 1530549124

Give feedback on the book at:
me@jennykellett.com

Printed in U.S.A

Introduction

Thank you for purchasing this book. In my life, positive quotes have had a huge influence on my motivation. It's incredible what a few words can do for you — it can take you from chronic procrastinator to achieving some of your greatest work. They are uplifting, inspiring and thought-provoking.

In this book, I have hand-picked 365 of my favorite motivational quotes — that's one for each day of the year. How you use this book is entirely up to you, but I find that it's worth grabbing a pen or some Post-It notes and marking the quotes that really resonate with you. Everyone is affected differently by different words — and also at different times of our lives, and when you find one that motivates you personally, you want to be able to access it whenever you're feeling flat.

Perhaps you want to pick some of your favorites, write them down and place them beside your bed, in your purse or next to your desk. Whatever works for you! You can also use the page on the right to take note of some of your favorites.

My motivational quotes...

"You simply have to put one foot in front of the other to keep going. Put blinders on and plow right ahead"

"If you don't design your own life plan, chances are you'll fall into someone else's plan. And guess what they have planned for you? Not much."

"Don't judge each day by the harvest you reap, but by the seeds you plant."

"Our greatest weakness lies in giving up. The most certain way to succeed is always to try just one more time."

"Nothing is impossible; the word itself says "I'm possible"!"

"You are never too old to set a new goal or dream another dream."

"Everyone wants to live at the top of the mountain, but all the happiness and growth occurs while you're climbing it."

"The best way to get something done is to begin."

"After a storm comes a calm."

"A year from now you may wish you had started today."

"You were born to win, but to be a winner, you must plan to win, prepare to win, and expect to win."

"If and When were planted, and Nothing grew."

"The tragedy of life doesn't lie in not reaching your goal. The tragedy lies in having no goal to reach."

"Do it now. Sometimes 'later' becomes never."

"Try not to become a man of success, but a man of value."

"As soon as you really commit to making something happen, the 'how' will reveal itself."

"Expect problems and eat them for breakfast."

"I don't believe you have to be better than everybody else. I believe you have to be better than you ever thought you could be."

"Dear tomorrow, do whatever you wanna do… I have already lived my today and I am not afraid of you anymore."

"People who are crazy enough to think they can change the world, are the ones who do."

"Energy flows where attention goes."

"Make your life a mission - not an intermission."

"Falling down is how we grow. Staying down is how we die."

"Even if you fall on your face, you're still moving forward."

"You can't cross the sea merely by standing and staring at the water."

"Success is not final, failure is not fatal: it is the courage to continue that counts."

"A river cuts through a rock not because of its power, but its persistence."

"If you can't stop thinking about it, don't stop working for it."

"The best way to predict the future is to create it."

"When you feel like quitting, think about why you started."

"Don't stop when you are tired. Stop when you are DONE."

"I believe in the person I want to become."

"Wake up with determination. Go to bed with satisfaction."

"In order to succeed, we must first believe that we can."

"If Plan A didn't work, the alphabet has 25 more letters."

"Mistakes are proof that you are trying."

"Nothing worth having comes easy."

"Work until your idols become your rivals."

"You only fail when you stop trying."

"Be stubborn about your goals, and flexible about your method."

"Do something today that your future self will thank you for."

"Don't count the days, make the days count."

"Your only limit is you."

"There is no elevator to success. You have to take the stairs."

"Sometimes you win; sometimes you learn."

"Believing in yourself is the first secret to success."

"Make today so awesome that tomorrow gets jealous."

"If you're going through hell, keep going."

"Push yourself, because no one else is going to do it for you."

"Stop being afraid of what could go wrong and start being positive about what could go right."

"Without hard work nothing grows but weeds."

"Strive for progress, not perfection."

"Fall seven times; stand up eight."

"Success all depends on the second letter."

"Life is 10% what happens to you, and 90% how you react."

"Don't watch the clock. Do what it does — keep on going."

"Knowing is not enough; we must apply. Willing is not enough; we must do."

"Be a warrior, not a worrier."

"The only way to do great work is to love what you do."

"When you want to succeed as much as you want to breathe, that's when you become successful."

"Persistence can change failure into extraordinary achievement."

"Yesterday you said tomorrow."

"Successful people never worry about what others are doing."

"I can't change the direction of the wind, but I can adjust my sails to always reach my destination."

"You can't have a better tomorrow if you're still thinking about yesterday."

"If you can find a path with no obstacles, it probably doesn't lead anywhere."

"Some days you just have to create your own sunshine."

"The expert in anything was once a beginner."

"Every accomplishment starts with the decision to try."

"Pressure can burst a pipe, but it can also create diamonds."

"Be a game changer; the world already has enough followers."

"Wake up. Kick ass. Repeat."

"Take a deep breath. It's just a bad day, not a bad life."

"Patience is not the ability to wait, but the ability to keep a good attitude while waiting."

"The only time you should ever look back is to see how far you have come."

"If the plan doesn't work, change the plan — not the goal."

"I don't know what the future holds, but I do know who holds the future."

"There are no secrets to success. It is the result of preparation, hard work and learning from failure."

"Strive not to be a success, but to be of value."

"Don't let the fear of losing be greater than the excitement of winning."

"Don't let small minds convince you that your dreams are too big."

"Quality means doing it right when no one is looking."

"Things do not happen. Things are made to happen."

"Strength doesn't come from what you can do. It comes from overcoming the things you once thought you couldn't do."

"Every champion was once a contender who refused to give up."

"If it doesn't challenge you, it doesn't change you."

"The dream is free. The hustle is sold separately."

"Today I will do what others won't, so tomorrow I can do what others can't."

"If opportunity doesn't knock, build a door."

"Go confidently in the direction of your dreams. Live the life you have imagined."

"What hurts more — the pain of hard work, or the pain of regret?"

"Keep away from those who try to belittle your ambitions."

"There is always room at the top."

"Every day is a second chance."

"Quit talking. Start doing."

"In the end, we only regret the chances we didn't take."

"No matter how you feel, get up, dress up, show up and never give up."

"Every job is a self-portrait of the person who does it. Autograph your work with excellence."

"Arriving at one goal is the starting point for another."

"A smooth sea never made a skillful sailer."

"Do your best and forget the rest."

"It always seems impossible until it's done."

"Think positive, and positive things will happen."

"Slow progress is better than no progress."

"Be yourself and quit trying to be everyone else."

"Courage is taking those first steps to your dream. Even if you can't see the path ahead."

"To live is the rarest thing on Earth. Most people just exist."

"Don't quit. Suffer now and live the rest of your life as a champion."

"Whatever the mind can conceive and believe, it can achieve."

"The future belongs to those who believe in the beauty of their dreams."

"It's not about being the best, it's about being better than you were yesterday."

"Do it because they said you couldn't."

"Either you run the day or the day runs you."

"You are only confined by the walls you build yourself."

"I'm not here to be average. I'm here to be awesome."

"Your life is your message to the world. Make sure it's inspiring."

"There is no "I" in team, but there is in win."

"Life begins at the end of your comfort zone."

"Make today ridiculously amazing."

"Whenever anyone has offended me, I try to raise my soul so high that the offense can not reach it."

"What would you attempt to do if you knew you could not fail?"

"The distance between your dream and reality is called action."

"Be so busy improving yourself that you have no time to criticize others."

"Life is too short to wait."

"Education is the most powerful weapon we can use to change the world."

"Be the type of person you want to meet."

"A motivated man is motivated by the desire to achieve, not by the desire to beat others."

"Most powerful is he who has himself in his own power."

"There is no one giant step. It's lots of little steps."

"Enjoy the little things in life… for one day you'll look back and realize they were the big things."

"You can't put a limit on anything."

"Chop your own wood and it will warm you twice."

"You'll be surprised to know how far you can go from the point where you thought it was the end."

"Some people create their own storms, then get upset when it rains."

"Always end the day with a positive thought."

"Wake up, smile and tell yourself today is my day."

"The best is yet to come."

"Only in the darkness can you see the stars."

"Your mind is a powerful thing. When you fill it with positive thoughts, your life will start to change."

"Surround yourself by people who are going to lift you higher."

"Do the difficult things when they are easy and do the great things while they are small."

"In order to carry a positive action, we must develop here a positive vision."

"Happiness can be found, even in the darkest of times, if one only remembers to turn on the light."

"Confidence is not 'They will like me', it's 'I'll be fine if they don't'."

"It may be stormy now, but it never rains forever."

"Negative people need drama like oxygen. Stay positive, it will take their breath away."

"You have 86,400 seconds today. How will you use them?"

"Those who don't believe in magic will never find it."

"Be the change you want to see in the world."

"You can't appreciate the good days without the bad ones."

"Stop looking for happiness in the same place you lost it."

"You are stronger than you seem, braver than you believe, and smarter than you think you are."

"One small positive thought in the morning can change your entire day."

"When everything seems like an uphill struggle, just think of the view from the top."

"Talking about our problems is our greatest addiction. Break the habit. Talk about your joys."

"One kind word can change someone's entire day."

"We may encounter many defeats, but we must not be defeated."

"Challenges are what make life interesting, and overcoming them is what makes life meaningful."

"Your mistakes do not define you."

"Be in love with your life."

"You were given this life because you were strong enough to live it."

"Success is how high you bounce when you hit the bottom."

"Try and fail.
Don't fail to try."

"The darkest hour has only 60 minutes."

"Be proud of who you are and not ashamed of how someone else sees you."

"A certain darkness is needed to see the stars."

"Turn your can'ts into cans and your dreams into plans."

"You can't live a positive life with a negative mind."

"Life is your mirror. What you see as your outside always comes from the inside."

"There is no passion to be found in settling for a life that is less than you are capable of living."

"Be so good they can't ignore you."

"Take time today to appreciate someone who does something you take for granted."

"The happiest people don't have the best of everything, they just make the most of everything."

"Life's a journey, not a race."

"If everybody likes what you're doing, you're doing it wrong."

"Don't be afraid of change, it is leading you to a new beginning."

"Worry less, giggle more."

"Don't chase people; be you. Do your own thing and work hard. The right people who belong in your life will come to you. And stay."

"Some people dream of success, while others wake up and work hard for it."

"You'll never change your life until you change something you do daily. The secret of your success is found in your daily routine."

"There is only one corner of the universe you can be certain of improving, and that's your self."

"The greatest pleasure in life is doing what others say you cannot do."

"The past should be the past. It can destroy the future. Live life for what tomorrow has to offer, not for what yesterday has taken away."

"Don't worry about those who talk behind your back. They're behind you for a reason."

"It's OK to be a glowstick. Sometimes we have to break before we shine."

"Courage is what it takes to stand up and speak. Courage is also what it takes to sit down and listen."

"If you don't go after what you want, you will never have it. If you don't ask, the answer will always be no. If you don't step forward, you're always in the same place."

"The struggle you're in today is developing the strength you need for tomorrow."

"Any intelligent fool can make things bigger and more complex… it takes a touch of genius — and a lot of courage — to move in the opposite direction."

"Trust yourself. You know more than you think you do."

"I'm going to make the rest of my life, the best of my life."

"Don't look back — you're not going that way."

"There will be obstacles, there will be doubters, there will be mistakes. But with hard work, there are no limits."

"All roads that lead to success have to pass through hardwork boulevard first."

"Don't give up what you want most for what you want now."

"If you are waiting for the right time, it's now."

"You only live once? False. You live everyday. You only die once."

"Unless you puke, faint or die — keep on going."

"You don't need a reason to help people."

"What's stopping you? That's right — nothing."

"Victory belongs to the most persevering."

"You're a diamond, dear. They can't break you."

"Worrying does not empty tomorrow of its troubles. It empties today of its strength."

"Don't let anyone dull your sparkle."

"Forget all the reasons why it won't work and believe the one reason why it will."

"Nobody makes you angry, you decide to use anger as a response."

"Inhale the good shit, exhale the bullshit."

"Think like a proton and stay positive."

"Keep your eyes on the stars and your feet on the ground."

"Stressed spelled backwards is dessert."

"You don't always need a plan. Sometimes you just need to breathe, trust, let go, and see what happens."

"Positive mind. Positive vibes. Positive life."

"Believe that life is worth living and your belief will help create the fact."

"Fear kills more dreams than failure ever will."

"The creative adult is the child who survived."

"You can't start the new chapter of your life if you keep re-reading the last one."

"When one door of happiness closes, another opens; but often we look so long at the closed doors that we do not see the one which has been opened for us."

"Life is all about finding people who are your kind of crazy."

"I'm just human. I have weaknesses, I make mistakes, and I experience sadness. But I learn from all these things to make me a better person."

"Think a little less. Live a little more."

"Count your blessings, not your problems."

"Every thought we think is creating our future."

"Right now, someone out there is wondering what it's like to know someone like me."

"If someone is strong enough to bring you down, show them you're strong enough to get back up."

"Life is like photography. We develop from the negatives."

"Life isn't about waiting for the storm to pass... it's learning to dance in the rain."

"My desire to succeed is more powerful than disappointment."

"Every day there is sad news and bad news, but each day itself is glad news."

"Life can be unfair sometimes, but that's no reason to give up on it."

"Dream without fear; live without limits."

"It doesn't matter who hurt you, or broke you down. What matters is who made you smile again."

"Let your smile change the world, but don't let the world change your smile."

"A wish changes nothing. A decision changes everything."

"Even too much sunshine can be devastating, while only with rain can growth occur. Accept both as part of the growing process in the garden of life."

"Everything will be OK in the end. If it's not OK, it's not the end."

"When someone walks out of your life, let them. They're just making room for someone better to walk in."

"There are two ways of spreading light — to be the candle, or the mirror that reflects that."

"Ships in harbours are safe, but that's not what ships were built for."

"The past is where you learned the lesson, the future is where you apply the lesson. Don't give up in the middle."

"Don't let insecurity ruin the beauty you were born with."

"Good, better, best. Never let it rest. 'Til good is better and your better is best."

"When you reach the end of your rope, tie a knot in it and hang on."

"Don't follow the crowd, let the crowd follow you."

"Positive thinking creates a doorway through which angels love to walk."

"Respect yourself enough to walk away from anything that no longer serves you, grows you or makes you happy."

"Don't look back — you might fall over what is right in front of you."

"Before you point the finger, make sure your hands are clean."

"Better than a thousand hollow words, is one word that brings peace."

"I've learned so much from my mistakes... that I'm thinking of making some more."

"Dream, but always with your eyes wide open."

"If you can't stand for something, you will fall for anything."

"A smile is the cheapest way to improve your looks, even if your teeth are crooked."

"Live without pretending, love without depending, listen without defending and speak without offending."

"Never wait for the perfect moment. Use the moment and make it perfect."

"Sacrifice is willing to give up something good for something better."

"Pain is temporary, quitting is forever."

"What goes around, comes around. Keep your circle positive."

"Happiness is putting more effort into your intentions rather than your expectations."

"Live as if you were going to die tomorrow. Learn as if you were to live forever."

"A strong positive mental attitude will create more miracles than any wonder drug."

"Accept the challenges so that you can feel the exhilaration of victory."

"Teach the triple truth to all: A generous heart, kind speech, and a life of service and compassion are the things which renew humanity."

"Be positive, patient and persistent."

"Without love, we are birds with broken wings."

"You know you have everything when you have nothing to lose."

"Yesterday's the past, tomorrow's the future, but today is the gift. That's why they call it the present."

"Happiness is the selling of the soul into its most appropriate spot."

"The difference between a successful person and others is not a lack of strength, not a lack of knowledge, but rather a lack of will."

"Imperfection is beauty. Madness is genius. And it's better to be absolutely ridiculous than absolutely boring."

"Without peace, all other dreams vanish and are reduced to ashes."

"Not all who wander are lost."

"The journey is the reward."

"Learn from yesterday, live for today, hope for tomorrow. The important thing is not to stop questioning."

"People may doubt what you say, but they'll believe what you do."

"Focus. Determination. Domination."

"Showing your emotions is a sign of strength."

"Let us sacrifice today so that our children can have a better tomorrow."

"Health is the greatest gift, contentment the greatest wealth, faithfulness the best relationship."

"I CAN is a thousand times more important than IQ."

"Success consists of doing the common things of life uncommonly well."

"Open your eyes, look within. Are you satisfied with the life you're living?"

"Positive thinking evokes more energy, more initiative, more happiness."

"Do not wait for leaders, do it alone — person to person."

"A leader is a dealer in hope."

"If your actions inspire others to dream more, learn more, do more and become more, you are a leader."

"Too many people overvalue what they are not and undervalue what they are."

"Ability is what you are capable of doing, motivation determines what you do. Attitude determines how well you do it."

"Efforts and courage are not enough without purpose and direction."

"A miracle is a shift in perception from fear to love."

"You have the power to feel any way you choose. So choose to feel wonderful."

"Dreams don't work unless you do."

"Before asking someone why they hate you, ask yourself why you even really care."

"We judge ourselves by what we feel capable of doing, while others judge us by what we have already done."

"Never apologize for showing feelings. By doing so, you apologize for the truth."

"Life is infinitely stranger than anything the mind could invent."

"Some relationships are like glass. It is better to leave it broken than to hurt yourself more by trying to put it back together."

"Keep smiling and one day life will get tired of upsetting you."

"If you expect the world to be fair with you because you are fair, you're fooling yourself. That's like expecting the lion not to eat you because you didn't eat him."

"It is perfectly OK to admit you're not OK."

"The strongest people are not those who show strength in front of us, but those who win battles we know nothing about."

"Life is a strange game. The only winning move is not to play."

"The naked truth is always better than the best-dressed lie."

"The only words you'll regret more than the ones left unsaid are the ones you used to intentionally hurt someone."

"Things will get worse before they get better. But when they do, remember who put you down, and who helped you up."

"Enjoy life now. This is not a rehearsal."

"A second chance doesn't mean anything if you haven't learned from your first mistake."

"Weak people revenge. Strong people forgive. Intelligent people ignore."

"People wait all week for Friday, all year for summer, all life for happiness."

"Respect people who find time for you in their busy schedule, but love people who never look at their schedule when you need them."

"Your past is just a story. And once you realize this, it has no power over you."

"Forgive them and forget them. Holding onto anger and bitterness consumes you not them."

"Greatness is best measured by how well an individual responds to the happenings in life that appear to be totally unfair, unreasonable, and undeserved."

"It's not about what you've done, it's about what you're doing. It's all about where you're going, no matter where you've been."

"Life is long. There will be pain but life goes on with everyday a brand new song."

"A journey of a thousand miles begins with a single step."

"Why have regrets? Everything that's going to happen to you is going to happen."

"Let your light shine. Be a source of strength and courage. Share your wisdom. Radiate love."

"When you try and control everything, you enjoy nothing. Relax, breathe, let go and live."

"You can run away from your problems just as easily as you can escape your shadow."

"Millions of people can believe in you, yet none of it matters unless you believe in yourself."

"When life gives you something that makes you feel afraid, that's when life gives you a chance to grow strong and be brave."

"When someone else's happiness is your happiness, that is love."

"Accept what you can't change, and change what you can't accept."

"Everything you've ever wanted is on the other side of fear."

"Anyone can be cool, but awesome takes practice."

"The very best motivation is yourself."

"If everyone practiced being who they are instead of pretending to be who they aren't, there would be peace."

"Everything happens for a reason. Maybe you don't see the reason right now, but when it is finally revealed it will blow you away."

"If you don't cut a cake, it's only one slice."

"Creativity is intelligence having fun."

"Not everything in life comes in handy, so don't expect to get everything easily."

"If we don't know our own worth, then we shouldn't expect someone to calculate it for us."

"Love doesn't hurt, expectations do."

"Life is too short to worry about stupid things. Have fun. Fall in love. Regret nothing, and don't let people bring you down."

"Sometimes I pretend to be normal, but it gets boring. So I go back to being me."

"People only rain on your parade because they're jealous of your sun and tired of their shade."

"Be strong enough to let go and wise enough to wait for what you really deserve."

"Sometimes the people with the best advice are the ones with the most problems."

"If you don't know what direction you're going, how will you know when you go off course?"

"As we grow older, we realize what we need to leave behind."

"Break the rules, stand apart. Ignore your head, follow your heart."

"Visualize your victory."

"When you're happy you enjoy the music, when you're sad you understand the lyrics."

"Life is a pure flame, and we live by an invisible sun within us."

"Don't limit yourself to the skies when there is a whole galaxy out there."

"Stay positive and the ups will be more frequent than the downs."

"Very little is needed to make a happy life; it is all within yourself, in your way of thinking."

"By being yourself, you put something wonderful in the world that wasn't there before."

"Be so happy that when others look at you they become happy too."

"Hold the vision, trust the process."

"Follow your dreams. They know the way."

"Think happy thoughts and put a smile on your face so that positive opportunities can find you."

"The greatest weapon against stress is the ability to choose one thought over another."

"People change and often, they become the person they said they will never be."

"Think of all the beauty still left around you, and be happy."

"You only live once, so think twice."

"All my life I have tried to pluck a thistle and plant a flower wherever the flower would grow in thought and mind."

"Everything in your life is a reflection of a choice you have made. If you want a different result, make a different choice."

"If you can't be a pencil to write anyone's happiness, then try to be an eraser to remove someone's sadness."

"No matter how good or bad you think life is, wake up each day and be thankful for life. Someone somewhere is fighting to survive."

"If you have good thoughts they will shine out of your face like sunbeams and you will always look lovely."

"You are allowed to be both a masterpiece and a work in progress simultaneously."

"Life doesn't always give you second chances, so take the first one."

"You cannot stop the waves, but you can learn to surf."

"You will never get what you truly deserve if you remain attached to what you're supposed to let go of."

"The key is to keep company only with people who uplift you, whose presence calls forth your best."

Manufactured by Amazon.ca
Bolton, ON